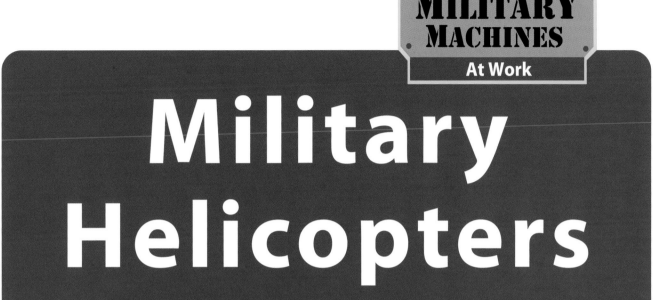

Military Helicopters

MILITARY MACHINES
At Work

By E. S. Budd

The Child's World®, Inc.

Published by The Child's World®, Inc.
PO Box 326
Chanhassen, MN 55317-0326
800-599-READ
www.childsworld.com

Design and Production:
The Creative Spark, San Juan Capistrano, CA

Photos: © 2002 David M. Budd Photography
        Pages 10 (right) and 11 are courtesy of the United States Army.

We thank the personnel at Fort Carson (Colorado Springs, CO)
for their help and cooperation in preparing this book.

Library of Congress Cataloging-in-Publication Data

Budd, E. S.
Military helicopters / by E.S. Budd.
      p. cm.
ISBN 1-56766-981-6
1. Military helicopters—Juvenile literature.
[1. Military helicopters. 2. Helicopters.]   I. Title.
UG1230 .B84 2001
623.7'46047—dc21
                            2001000338

Contents

On the Job

On the job, military helicopters can **transport** soldiers and **cargo** quickly. Sometimes military helicopters are used in battle. Other times, they are used to rescue injured or sick people. Military helicopters can be used like flying **ambulances.**

4

This helicopter has two pilots.

They sit in the **cockpit.**

The **cabin** can carry other people. Rescue helicopters have room for up to 6 **patients.**

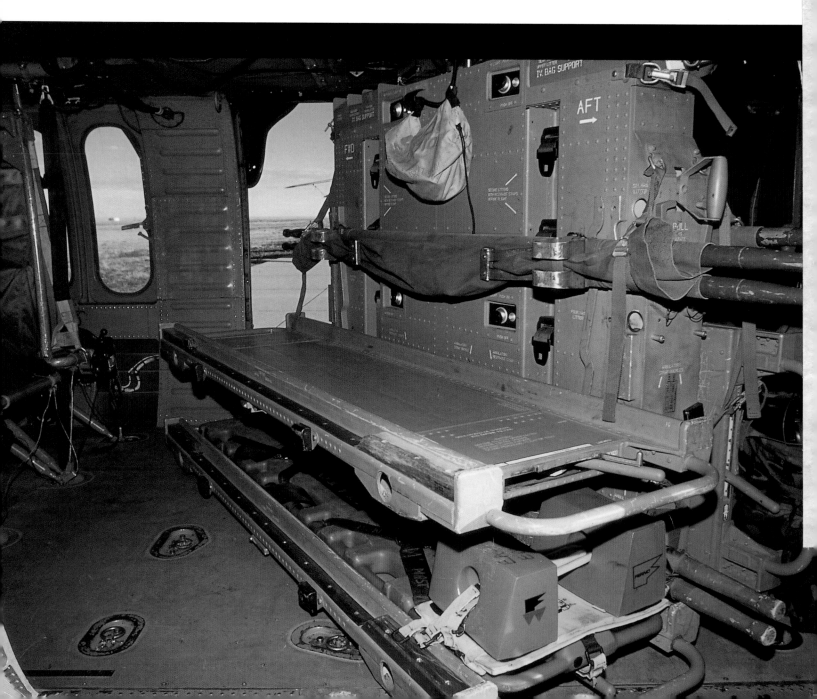

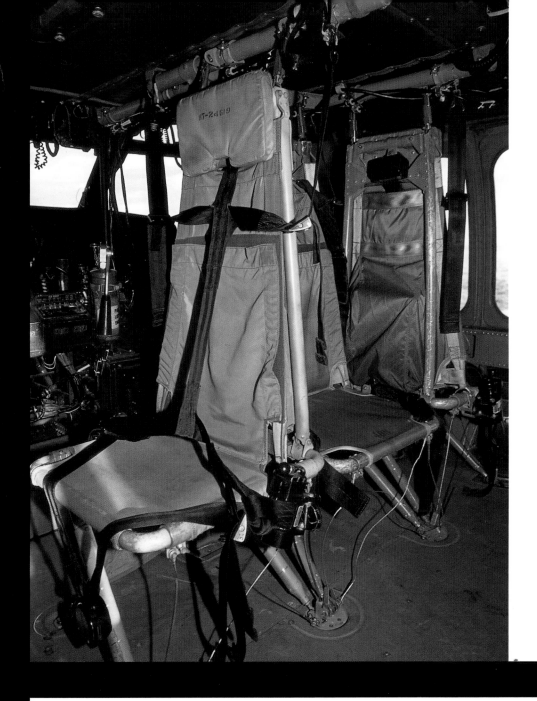

Other helicopters can carry up to

12 **passengers.**

Military helicopters have a **hoist.** It can safely lift an injured person into the helicopter. Ropes can lower a soldier from the helicopter to the ground.

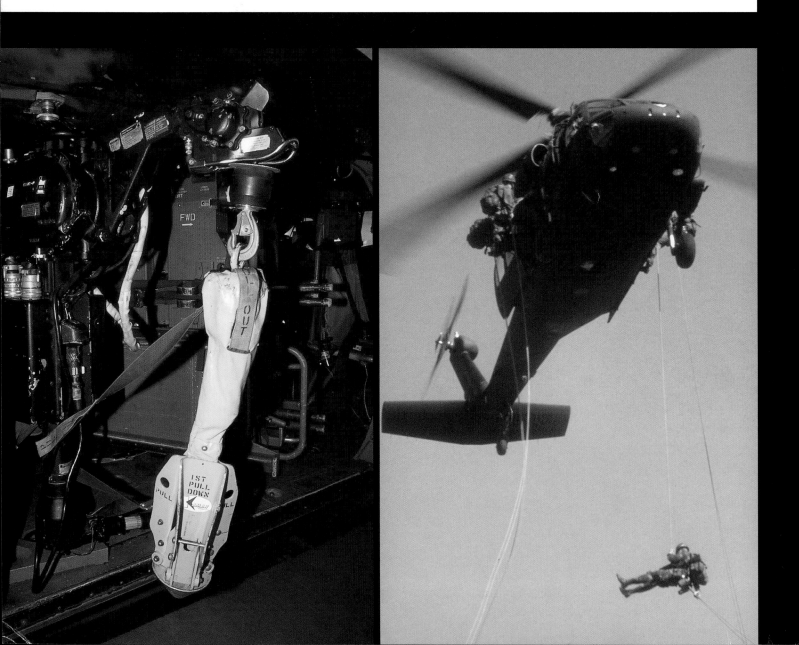

Military helicopters can even lift very

heavy things, such as trucks.

A military helicopter has **rotors** on top. The rotors spin around and around. They move very fast to make the helicopter fly.

There is another rotor on the helicopter's tail. It helps the helicopter fly straight.

Stabilizers on the tail make the ride smooth.

Now it's time for takeoff. The pilots make

sure everything is ready to go.

Climb Aboard!

Would you like to see where the pilot sits?

Controls help the pilot steer the helicopter.

They also help the pilot take off and land.

Up Close

The inside   1. The pilot's seat

                                    2. The controls

The cockpit

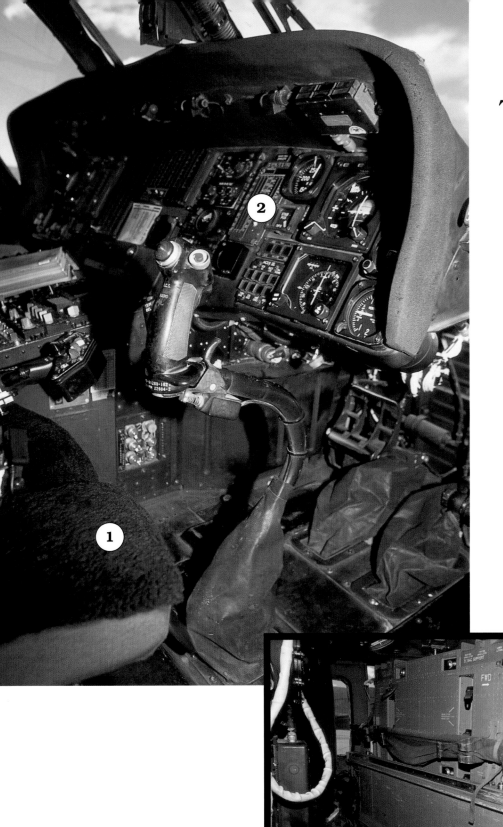

The cabin

The outside

1. The stabilizers

2. The rotors

3. The cabin

4. The cockpit

Glossary

ambulances (AM-byoo-len-sez)
Ambulances are vehicles that are used to carry sick or injured people. Military helicopters can be used as flying ambulances.

cabin (KAB-en)
A cabin is the open space inside a helicopter. Cargo and passengers are carried in the cabin.

cargo (KAR-goh)
Cargo is a load of goods carried by a vehicle. A military helicopter can carry cargo.

cockpit (KOK-pit)
A cockpit is the place where the pilot of an airplane or helicopter sits. A pilot flies a military helicopter from the cockpit.

controls (kun-TROHLZ)
Controls are buttons, switches, and other tools that make a machine work. A pilot uses controls to fly a military helicopter.

hoist (HOYST)
A hoist is a tool used to lift heavy loads. A military helicopter has a hoist.

passengers (PASS-en-jerz)
Passengers are people who travel in vehicles. Some military helicopters have room for 12 passengers.

patients (PAY-shents)
Patients are people who need medical care. A military helicopter can transport patients to a hospital.

rotors (ROH-terz)
Rotors are long metal parts on a helicopter. Rotors spin around very quickly to move a helicopter through the air.

stabilizers (STAY-buh-lie-zerz)
Stabilizers are metal parts on the tail of a helicopter. They make a helicopter fly more smoothly.

transport (TRAN-sport)
To transport something means to carry it from one place to another. A military helicopter can transport soldiers and cargo quickly.